TABLE OF CONTENTS

Unless otherwise indicated bible quotations are from
https://www.biblegateway.com/ amplified Bible.

©Lavene Lee Elliott
2022 Destiny Tribe LLC

BREAKING THE POWER OF DEMONIC SUGGESTIONS

For humans, language is a form of symbolic communication, and semantic input can provoke both cognitive and sensory emotional responses. Speaking, writing and reading are integral to everyday life, where language is the primary tool for expression and communication. Words have the potential to bind and loose, uplift or suppress our emotions.

A suggestion is an idea or plan put forward for consideration. It is the process by which a physical or mental state is influenced by a thought or idea. It is an extension of the mechanism of communication. Suggestion is also a psychological tool used in behavioural science to aid in modifying behaviour, or an experience.

Something is considered demonic when it is resembling, or has characteristics of demons or evil spirits.

What is demonic suggestions? It is the process by which a physical, mental or spiritual state is influenced by a demonically implanted, or empowered thought, idea or feeling.

Suggestion may be imaginary or abstract. The imagination is considered "a power of the mind," "a creative faculty of the mind," "the mind" itself when in use, and a process used for thinking, scheming, contriving, remembering, creating, fantasizing, and forming opinion. I strongly believe that the imagination is the first introduction we have to the spirit realm.

The imagination is located in the intangible realm or what is often refer to as the invisible realm. We may have heard a child talking to an imaginary friend, or partaking in an imaginary event, which is so real to the child that he/she may not be able to differentiate what is imaginative from that of reality.

Hebrew 11:3 says By faith [that is, with an inherent trust and enduring confidence in the power, wisdom and goodness of God] we understand that the worlds (universe, ages) were framed *and* created [formed, put in order, and equipped for their intended purpose] by the word of God, so that what is seen was not made out of things which are visible.

The spirit realm holds the truth to what will eventually be our reality on a day to day level of manifestation. The mind and intellect is the content of the soul thus experiencing any form of alteration ,or negative influence within the mind will have a direct impact on what we believe, think, and feel.

The adversary imposes his thoughts, ideas and evil plans to influence our thoughts and feelings. Demonic suggestions are thoughts and sensual feelings that are demonically planted and stated that makes an impact on the conscious or the sub-conscious mind in one's sleeping our waking state. Have you ever had a dream in which it was so real that you cannot differentiate reality from the dream, or have someone ever suggested something to you wherein it took you a moment to work out whether or not what was "suggested" was a reality?

I believe that the years 2021& 2022 have been thought provoking years. Never have we been so much alone with our thoughts or the thoughts of others. We have seen the birthing of many creators during the pandemic, but we have also seen an overwhelming rise in mental health and mental issues. I believe these last two years has been a blessing and a curse to many. There are those who hated to be left alone with their thoughts, while others seized the moment to becoming creators.

There are some experiences that have defined my outlook on the power of suggestions.

Whilst this E-Book is on the power of demonic suggestions bear in mind that suggestions in and of itself is a tool that can be used for good or evil. I recounted the year 2021 I was in New York this was one of the most defining moments for me. I often struggled with feelings of anxiety.

The anxiety I experienced over the years could be as simple as a phone call from a bill collector or having to meet someone, or fulfill a ministry assignment. I can recall in the passed having a fail marriage and was called on a ministry assignment and turned down the opportunity based on the fact that I couldn't face the crowd or was too afraid to be asked of my marital status. Or my landlord would send me a message requesting a meeting and that would be a trigger for me. What I felt over the years have been so severe that it caused my hair to fall out.

As I recounted the New York experience. It was such an alarming experience wherein I found myself crying everyday. The anxiety would start as I heard the garage door open, or when I heard loud or quarrelsome tones, or if I was invited to eat out. It was almost any and everything. Whilst this time was disturbing for me I also deemed it a time of healing in that the Lord would have revealed to me the root cause of the fear and anxiety I was experiencing.

That morning I woke up crying, my daughter and myself was sharing the same room. As I utter tiny outburst of prayers I felt that my soul was overwhelmed, and bursting at it's seams.

In a vision I was brought back to my great-grandmothers house. In the dream I was a child of about nine year old I found myself with my back against the wall trying to make my way into the house without being seen. (throughout my life I have always been trying not to be seen not knowing the root of it), as I pushed against the wall I finally made it into the house. By this time I was now hearing people chattering and my mother's voice was distinct from the others. I laid on the bed and listened but was also overwhelmed of being called. I woke from the dream with a clear sense that that vision was insight to the root and source of my fear and anxiety. God wants us to be whole in mind, body and spirit.

Backdrop

My grandmother's house was always a safe haven for me even though much of the trauma I experienced as a child took place in that environment. Her love language was never vocal, but was demonstrated in acts of kindness and gestures of service and care. I left my parents house when I was about 11 years old or perhaps younger. There were periods of intermissions when I would seem to be living with my mother, and father and other periods where I was seemingly living with my grand-Mother. Give and take my haven was my grandmother. There was always the fear that my mother was coming to take me home. Home was not a bad place but in my mind it wasn't where I wanted to be as a child, hence the vision mentioned above would reveal my psychological convictions of where home was and what was safe. This dream activated my road to healing.

THE POWER OF SUGGESTIONS

Every one of our thoughts, good or bad, becomes concrete, materializes, and becomes in short a reality. Emile Coue.

What is the power of suggestion? The power of suggestion is when an individual has an idea conveyed to them, and that idea, in turn, becomes reality. It is an instrument used to modify behaviour.

One of the most powerful tool used in communication is the voice. Language is not just having a voice but rather what comes out of that voice or the impact that a voice makes in our lives. We have lived our lives based on the influence of language. Our voices matter as much as our words matter. They have the power to awaken the senses and lead others to act, close deals, or land us successful job interviews. Your mother ,teacher, or boss voice means something to you.

Language is an expression of our beliefs and culture. If a person believes in an expected outcome, they are more likely to automatically achieve that outcome. This is the basis for the power of suggestion. This phenomenon is used in psychology and healthcare to greatly improve the lives of people but can also be manipulated to cause pain and torture.

SUBLIMINAL MESSAGES

A *subliminal message* is a technique used in marketing and other media to influence people without them being aware of what the messenger is doing. This may involve the use of split second flashes of text, hidden images, or subtle cues that affect a person at a level below conscious awareness. Subliminal messages used under demonic influence are intended to deceived, and sustain seasons of bondage, and hardship.

Deception is falsehood and can be introduced subliminally; through acts or statements that misleads, hides the truth, or promotes a belief, concept, or idea that is not true. The devil's playground is deception.

I MAGINATIONS
Someone once says;"**thoughts are things**" but I believe thoughts become things.

"The imagination bridges the gap between images and ideas, implying that rational thought takes place in the form of images, and are stored and combined in the imagination. Thus, imagination is implied as an actual space or medium in the individual's mind, and in this space it has a power to combine images and ideas to do the work of reason."

2 Corinthians 10:5 Casting down imaginations, "destroying sophisticated arguments" and every exalted *and* proud thing that sets itself up against the [true] knowledge of God, and *we are* taking every thought *and* purpose captive to the obedience of Christ,

Hebrew 11:3 says By faith [that is, with an inherent trust and enduring confidence in the power, wisdom and goodness of God] we understand that the worlds (universe, ages) were framed *and* created [formed, put in order, and equipped for their intended purpose] by the word of God, so that what is seen was not made out of things which are visible.

We form worlds, and spaces through images and ideas hence using our imagination.This is particularly effective especially if you are able to manipulate your own "good thoughts" so as to produce an intended result. In fact the faculty of imagination is used in counselling and hypnosis to counter addictive traps, etc. Imagination and the use of it could be consider neutral especially when it is free from external influences. The problem is when imaginations are influenced by an external or demonic forces.The spirit of fear and anxiety takes advantage of our imaginations. It seeks to find expression through that medium so as to keep us in cycles off oppression.

I DENTIFYING THE SPIRIT OF DEMONIC SUGGESTIONS Every demonic suggestion begins with a demonic conversation.

Let's take an example of demonic suggestions in Genesis 3:3… except the fruit from the tree which is in the middle of the garden. God said, 'You shall not eat from it nor touch it, otherwise you will die…"You will not certainly die," the serpent said to the woman. "For God knows that when you eat from it your eyes will be opened, and you will be like God, knowing good and evil."When the woman saw that the fruit of the tree was good for food and pleasing to the eye, and also desirable for gaining wisdom, she took some and ate it. She also gave some to her husband, who was with her, and he ate it.

Suggestions are so powerful even though they aren to actual facts, in fact they can actually create false memories in peoples lives even false memories of previous lives.

We don't know how long after the couple had the demonic suggestion planted in their minds that they acted on the desire but we know they did, and that resulted him them creating a "whole new world" literally.

A suggestion planted in the mind, given the right amount of care and attention will blossom into a whole new reality or a whole new life. It can even make someone believe they are someone they are not. A suggestion can be triggered at any moment.

Demonic suggestions are chaotic and deadly. They can potentially produce death in an individual. You can be paralyzed from head to toe by a demonic suggestion.

I had an experience not so long ago of someone telling me of an event that happen in my life (which in fact didn't happen). The person said; "I know of the time you did this". As I listened I progressively discovered that this suggestion was demonic and that it had originated out of hell, and also that its assignment was aimed at opening up an ugly season in my life.

Let's dissect the snare.
Thought process: like Eve I listened , I also analyzed the information and processed it. This process demands that we carefully discern the information that is being presented to us.
Immediately when I realized that what was suggested was demonic I rejected it. There were are actual facts of me being in the place mentioned
There was no fact or truth of me doing what I was accused of doing.

THE EFFECTS OF SUGGESTION

Identifying Triggers

In more recent times we have been hearing the term triggers more and more. Triggers are not new however they are very real experiences. In mental health triggers refers to something that affects your emotional state, in most state significantly that it may cause you to become extremely overwhelmed or distressed. It affects your ability to be present in that given moment, it may also bring up specific thoughts patterns or even influence one's behaviour.

Triggers are re-experienced symptoms of trauma when exposed to reminders. They vary widely and could be internal or external. Specific phrases, such as odours, or sounds can all be triggers for people who have experienced traumatic events such as: rape, physical assault, emotional abuse, spiritual abuse ,loss of a loved one, etc.

I mentioned earlier my experience in New York and how I was affected by fear and anxiety which started manifesting at a certain hour of the day and at the sound of the garage door opening. Those were the triggers the enemy was using to distract me from my ministry assignment. What is important to mention is that these triggers are manifestations of trauma or suggestions that have been implanted in the mind which may manifest at anytime. From a spiritual standpoint we are made aware that anxiety is a spirit. "For God has not given us a spirit of fear, but of power and of love and of a sound mind" 2 Timothy 1;7.

SATAN AND CIRCUMSTANCES

The devil is the father of lies and his native language is lie. The enemy will use circumstances and trauma to plant triggers within our minds that can leave us feeling paralyzed and defeated by a simple suggestion.

THE SPIRITUAL IMPLICATIONS OF DEMONIC SUGGESTIONS

OPEN DOORS

A door represents access points, an opening or an area in your life vulnerable to attack.

Matthew 12:43-45 says; at the return of an unclean Spirit When an "unclean spirit has gone out of a person, it passes through waterless places seeking rest, but finds none. Then it says, 'I will return to my house from which I came.' And when it comes, it finds the house empty, swept, and put in order. Then it goes and brings with it seven other spirits more evil than itself, and they enter and dwell there, and the last state of that person is worse than the first. So also will it be with this evil generation."

Evil is the opposite of good. The reality is that we are living in a time where there are so many access points to our minds that if we are not careful we become victims to the schemes of Satan. When we have opening in our lives we can become victims to the adversary. Doors can be open through conversations, images, access we give to media and media files, sexual immoralities, and items that are connected to the demonic realms, iniquitous patterns, generational curses, etc.

Demonization is a broad to topic as it relates to whether of not a believer can be demon possess. The focus is being demonically influence through conversations with demonic spirits. Any decision to engage in sinful practices or abominable things can open up one to demonic influence. This kind of influence can manifest through demonic deceivers for example someone professing to be a man or woman of God and more popularly someone proclaiming to be a prophet. Be careful of what, or whom you allow to access your mind.

It opens seasons of oppression and anxiety.
Ecclesiastes 7:7 Surely oppression maketh a wise man mad and a gift destroyeth the heart. Oppression does not always manifest in physical acts of pain and suffering, or impeding on human rights.One of the adversaries weapon of mass destruction is oppression.

Creates fear of the future
Demonic suggestion can potentially create fear of the future, and divine opportunities because of it's crippling effect. It can keep you trapped to the schemes of the devil. I will instruct you and teach you in the way you should go; I will counsel you [who are willing to learn] with My eye upon you.Psalm 32:8.

SUGGESTION MAY MANIFEST ITSELF IN ACCUSATION

Accusation is hard, brutal, and malicious, it is a spirit. The source of accusations is the accuser Satan. The spirit of accusation has multiple objectives. Its goal is to destroy you; then to destroy others; and ultimately destroy those around you so they can begin to operate under the same spirit with the same evil roots of bitterness. Accusation also cast doubt on God's word;For the accuser of our brethren, who accused them before our God day and night, has been cast down.Revelation 12:10-11. Be mindful that the accuser is cast down do not allow him to have dominion over your mind.

REJECTING DEMONIC SUGGESTIONS

COUNTER TRIGGERS

"For every action there's an equal and opposing reaction".

Counter is to take a contrary position. It is to go toward a different or opposite direction, result, or effect. The long-term impact of trauma lies in how it shapes our beliefs about other God, people, the world, and ourselves. The mind is a battle field where wars are won and subsequently lost depending on how trained, and prepare we are to fight.

There is no fair game when it comes on to the adversary. Satan is like a roaring lion seeking whom he may devourer. The rules of engagement gives us the picture of a word we use ever so often especially when dealing with falsehood or our counterfeit. When you identify a word, phrase or expression that interferes with your spirit immediately reject and ignore that word that has been placed in your mind.

PUSHBACK AND RESIST SUGGESTIONS

Secure your spiritual and physical atmosphere.
The adversary wants to rob you of your dominion and ultimately steal your possession which includes your joy and peace. There is a domain of rest that God wants us to enter in. The devil knows this and is therefore wants you to forfeit your place of rest. Secure your domain by keeping guard and protecting it.

One of the ways I protect my atmosphere is by keeping watch over my eyes and ears gates. I am very careful of what I allow to enter my atmosphere. Give no place to the devil...and do not give the devil an opportunity [to lead you into sin or bondage by holding a grudge, or nurturing anger, or harbouring resentment, or cultivating bitterness]. Ephesians 4:27

RENEW YOUR MIND

The battle over our minds goes way back to the Garden of Eden with Adam and Eve. For any type of performance and success , our mental, and spiritual training is just as important as the physical training as we do for any other type of discipline. Our interacting with information everyday can potentially take over our minds.

 The training and renewing of our minds is about doing it over and over again, applying the word daily and allowing it to modify and make our minds better and more in tune with God's will. What looks like perfection is an accumulation of repetitive practice and modification. We can use different techniques to make uncertainties more certain. We can build an internal policing system in our minds that can encourage us, and assist us in building a routine plan and or at times may instruct us or allow us to step back and strategize.

Do not be conformed to this world (this age), [fashioned after and adapted to its external, superficial customs], but be transformed (changed) by the [entire] renewal of your mind [by its new ideals and its new attitude], so that you may prove [for yourselves] what is the good and acceptable and perfect will of God, *even* the thing which is good and acceptable and perfect [in His sight for you].Romans 12:2

Breaking the power of demonic suggestions demands that we are led by the spirit and not by any other force or influence.(For as many as are led by the Spirit of God, they are the sons of God). Conformity to worldly wisdom, new age movements, or the philosophy of men is never the acceptable will of God for us.Romans 8:14.

Resisting suggestions involves counter triggering any implantation of control that the enemy has over us. James 4:7 says ; "So submit to [the authority of] God. Resist the devil [stand firm against him] and he will flee from you". We must recover grounds by taking control over our souls. Give no place to the devil.

Results of yielding to wrong person or attitudes. There are repercussions to us opening our minds to the wrong influence. **Romans. 6:16** says;"Know ye not, that to whom ye yield yourselves servants to obey, his servants ye are to whom ye obey; whether of sin unto death, or of obedience unto righteousness?".

One of the deceitfulness of trauma is that you feel as if the event or the experience is happening to you all over again in the moment. It's important that you become aware of where you are and the power of the present moment. Focus on right now, place your mindset in the present moment. Fill your thoughts with what's present, what's good and of a good report. Fill your mind with God's word and His goodness towards you.(For I know the thoughts that I think toward you, saith the Lord, thoughts of peace, and not of evil, to give you an expected end)Jeremiah 29;11.

FFIRMATIONS

I am enough. Before I was formed in my mothers womb God new me. I don't possess the need to be anything or anyone except that person I am created to be.

I do not need to be special. I am enough.

I am the one. There is no person with my skills, gifts and abilities that are unique to me.

I am chosen from my mother's womb.

I possess the mind of Christ in every area of my life.

I am loved. Jesus laid down is life for me. Greater love has no man than this.

I am more than a conqueror through Christ.

I am made whole through the blood of Jesus Christ.

But by the grace of God **I am what I am**: and his grace which was bestowed upon me was not in vain; but I laboured more abundantly than they all: yet not I, but the grace of God which was with me. 1 Corinthians 15:10.

PRAYER POINTS TO DISARM THE POWER OF DEMONIC SUGGESTIONS

Father in the name of Jesus the Christ;

- I now confess that I have the mind of Christ.

- I am seated in heavenly places with Christ Jesus far above principalities, and nothing by any means shall harm me. Ephesians 2:6

- Sin has no dominion over me.

- I confess that I am saved by the shed blood of Jesus Christ and the faculty of my mind is fully submitted to Christ and the word of God.

- Satan has no place in me or any claim on me.(I will not speak with you much longer, for the ruler of the world (Satan) is coming. And he has no claim on Me [no power over Me nor anything that he can use against Me)John 14;30.

- I will not suffer any torment or pain sanctioned by Satan. I reject torture and every spirit of torment.

- I resist bewitchment in the name of Jesus.

- I resist spells in the name of Jesus.

- I resist demonic triggers and every form of satanic suggestions placed in my mind whether consciously, or unconsciously in the name of Jesus.

- I resist demonic thoughts, and imaginations, anything, and every high thing that exalts itself about above the knowledge of God.

- I bring into captivity every thought to the obedience of Christ. 2 Corinthians 10:5

- I reject any thought that belittles who God said I am.

- I subject my mind only to the word of God that speaks to the good plans that He has for me. I think thoughts of peace and the laws of Christ.

- I break the power every word curse, pronouncements, demonic announcements, decrees and declarations in the name of Jesus Christ.

- I am not a slave to fear, anxiety or demonic suggestions. I yield only to the Lord Jesus Christ.

- My mind is governed by things that are true, whatsoever things are honest, whatsoever things are just, whatsoever things are pure, whatsoever things are lovely, whatsoever things are of good report in Jesus name.

- I submit myself to the Lordship of Jesus Christ.

- I am forgiven; for if the Son liberates me [makes you free men], then am I free. I confess that I am unquestionably free.

- I overcome by the blood of the Lamb and by the word of my testimony.

- I am healthy, emotionally, mentally, spiritually, and physically in Jesus name.

- Father Lord I thank you that you have release me from the terror of fear and anxiety.

- The blood of Jesus has release me from every stronghold in my soul.

- Now to Him Who, by (in consequence of) the [action of His] power that is at work within us, is able to [carry out His purpose and] do superabundantly, far over *and* above all that we [dare] ask or think [infinitely beyond our highest prayers, desires, thoughts, hopes, or dreams. Ephesians 3:20

SCRIPTURES TO HELP YOU IN YOUR COMBAT

Romans 12:2 - And be not conformed to this world: but be ye transformed by the renewing of your mind, that ye may prove what is that good, and acceptable, and perfect, will of God.

Be subject therefore unto God; but resist the devil, and he will flee from you. James 4;7.

Philippians 2:5 - Let this mind be in you, which was also in Christ Jesus:

Romans 8:1-39 - There is therefore now no condemnation to them which are in Christ Jesus, who walk not after the flesh, but after the Spirit.

Philippians 4:8 - Finally, brethren, whatsoever things are true, whatsoever things are honest, whatsoever things are just, whatsoever things are pure, whatsoever things are lovely, whatsoever things are of good report; if there be any virtue, and if there be any praise, think on these things.

Other books by Lavene Lee Elliott
TAKE ME TO MY LIFE
SWEET DREAMS OF DESTINY

Find us at
https://www.destinytribe.org

https://www.facebook.com/Lavenelee